Life Cycle of an

Oak Tree

Angela Royston

Heinemann Library
Chicago, Illinois

Designed by Celia Floyd
Illustrated by Alan Fraser
Printed by South China Printers in China

04 03 02 01
10 9 8 7 6 5 4 3 2

Library of Congress Cataloging-in-Publication Data
Royston, Angela.
    Life cycle of an oak tree / Angela Royston.
        p. cm.
    Includes bibliographical references (p.) and index.
    Summary: Introduces the life cycle of an oak tree, from the sprouting of an acorn
    through its more than 100 years of growth.
        ISBN 1-57572-211-9 (lib. bdg.)
        1. Oak—Life cycles—Juvenile literature. [1. Oak. 2. Trees.] I. Title.

QK495.F14R68 2000
583'.46—dc21   JJ 583.46   99-046855

Acknowledgments
The Publisher would like to thank the following for permission to reproduce photographs:

Ardea London, pp. 11; Ardea London/Bob Gibbons, p. 27; Ardea London/J. A. Bailey, p. 19;
Bruce Coleman Collection/Andrew Purcell, p. 12, Bruce Coleman Collection/Norbert Schwirtz,
p. 20; NHPA/Brian Hawkes, p. 18; NHPA/Daniel Heuclin, pp. 6, 7; NHPA/Roger Tidman, p. 17;
NHPA/Stephen Dalton, pp. 21, 24; Oxford Scientific Films/Alastair Shay, p. 22; Oxford Scientific
Films/Chris Sharp, p. 25; Oxford Scientific Films/Deni Bown, p. 15, Oxford Scientific Films/Niall
Benvie, p. 10; Oxford Scientific Films/Tim Shepherd, p. 4; Planet Earth Pictures/Rosemary
Calvert, p. 14; Wildlife Matters, pp. 5, 9, 16, 23, 26; Wildlife Matters/Sheila Apps, p. 13.

Cover photograph: Bruce Coleman

Every effort has been made to contact copyright holders of any material reproduced in this
book. Any omissions will be rectified in subsequent printings if notice is given to the Publisher.

Some words are shown in bold, **like this.** You can find out what they mean by looking in the glossary.

Contents

The Mighty Oak

There are thousands of different kinds of trees. You can tell them apart by the shape and color of their leaves.

Acorn

Sapling

Catkins

Every oak tree grows from a **seed** called an acorn. This book tells the story of how a mighty oak tree grew from one acorn.

New acorns   Adult oak   Old age

Acorn

The acorn has been lying in the ground in the forest all winter. In spring, the sun warms up the soil. The acorn begins to grow.

Acorn

Sapling

Catkins

A **root** grows down into the soil, and
a **shoot** pushes up through the ground.
The roots take in water from the soil,
and the leaves open.

New acorns

Adult oak

Old age

Sapling

The young tree is called a **sapling**.
The leaves use sunlight, air, and
water to make food for the tree.

Acorn Sapling Catkins

The food keeps the sapling alive
and helps it grow bigger and
stronger. It starts to grow twigs
and small branches.

New acorns   Adult oak   Old age

10

In autumn, the green leaves change color. Now they are red, yellow, and brown. They slowly dry up, die, and fall from the tree.

Acorn

Sapling

Catkins

New **buds** form on the tree, ready
to grow into leaves and twigs next
spring. The **sapling** and all the other
trees in the forest rest through the
cold winter.

New acorns

Adult oak

Old age

12

Every year the tree produces new leaves and twigs. It grows taller. The twigs become branches, and the trunk grows thicker.

Acorn

Sapling

Catkins

Now spring is coming again. New
buds are beginning to open in the
warm sun. These buds will form
new leaves.

New acorns

Adult oak

Old age

Catkins

The tree is covered in **catkins**. The long catkins are male. The wind blows the **pollen** from them onto the female flowers of another oak.

Acorn

Sapling

Catkins

These shorter catkins are female flowers. Some of the eggs in the female flowers join with grains of pollen to make new **seeds**.

New acorns

Adult oak

Old age

New Acorns

The new **seeds** swell and grow.
They become acorns. In autumn,
birds, squirrels, and other animals
eat the ripe acorns.

Acorn

Sapling

Catkins

Squirrels sometimes bury acorns to eat later but forget where they are. Some buried acorns may grow into new **saplings** next spring.

New acorns Adult oak Old age

Adult Oak

The tree has been alive as long as some people. Its trunk is tall and strong. Many kinds of animals live in the tree.

Acorn  Sapling Catkins

Several birds have built their nests among the leaves and twigs. Thousands of insects live in the **bark** and on the leaves.

New acorns   Adult oak   Old age

A **gall wasp** has laid its eggs under this leaf. The oak tree makes a special growth, or gall, around each egg. It is called an oak apple.

Acorn

Sapling

Catkins

The egg hatches into a **grub.** The grub eats the oak apple instead of the leaves. Now the grub has changed into a new gall wasp.

New acorns   Adult oak   Old age

A storm hits the forest. A mighty wind whips through the trees. Branches crack, and some of the trees are blown over.

Acorn   Sapling   Catkins

The top of the tree breaks off and crashes to the ground! But the rest of the tree is still alive, and it will keep on growing.

New acorns

Adult oak

Old age

Old Age

As long as it is alive, the tree never stops growing. Every year, new wood grows underneath the **bark**, and the trunk gets a little wider.

Acorn

Sapling

Catkins

Now the tree is hundreds of years old. The trunk is very wide, and the wood in the middle has rotted away. The trunk is **hollow**!

New acorns

Adult oak

Old age

Cutting the Trees

Oak trees can live for hundreds of years. Some die of disease. But most are cut down to make way for more roads and towns.

Acorn

Sapling

Catkins

Some of the trees are made into wood for furniture and houses. Some are made into logs that are burned in fireplaces.

New acorns   Adult oak   Old age

Life Cycle

Acorn growing

1

Sapling

2

Catkins

3

New acorns

4

Adult oak

5

Old age

6

Fact File

There are more than four hundred kinds of oak trees. Most oak trees can live for up to four hundred years. An English oak tree like the one in this book can live for as many as nine hundred years!

The **bark** of the cork oak is used to make corks for bottles and cork tiles. It used to be used inside life jackets to make them **float**.

Some oak galls are used to make inks and dyes. Some of the dyes are used in making leather.

Glossary

bark hard layer of wood that covers parts of a tree

bud small swelling on a tree that will grow into new leaves or flowers

catkin long group of flowers hanging from a tree branch

float to stay on top of water and not sink

gall wasp insect that lays eggs on oak trees

grub very young insect that looks like a worm

hollow empty

pollen fine powder made by male parts of plants

root part of a plant or tree that takes in water and food from the ground

sapling tiny young tree

seed part of a plant that is able to grow into a new plant

shoot tiny plant that is sent out from a seed and that will grow into an adult tree

More Books to Read

Bryant-Mole, Karen. *Trees.* Austin, Tex.: Raintree Steck-Vaughn, 1996.

Giesecke, Ernestine. *Trees.* Des Plaines, Ill.: Heinemann Library, 1998.

National Wildlife Federation Staff. *Trees Are Terrific!* Broomall, Penn.: Chelsea House, 1998.

Index